Arthurian Matters of Britain

Lion fountain at Chalice Well in Glastonbury

Mahmoud Shelton

Arthurian Matters of Britain

Celtic - Christian - Islamic

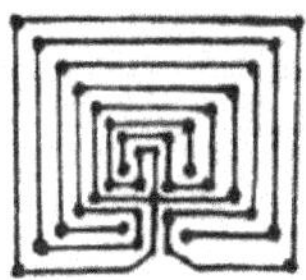

Temple of Justice Books

templeofjustice@icloud.com

Printed in the United States of America

ISBN 978-0-9741468-8-1

CONTENTS

The Knight of the Lion: Celtic and Islamic Elements

Custodians of the Grail

The Green Man King

The Knight of the Lion: Celtic and Islamic Elements

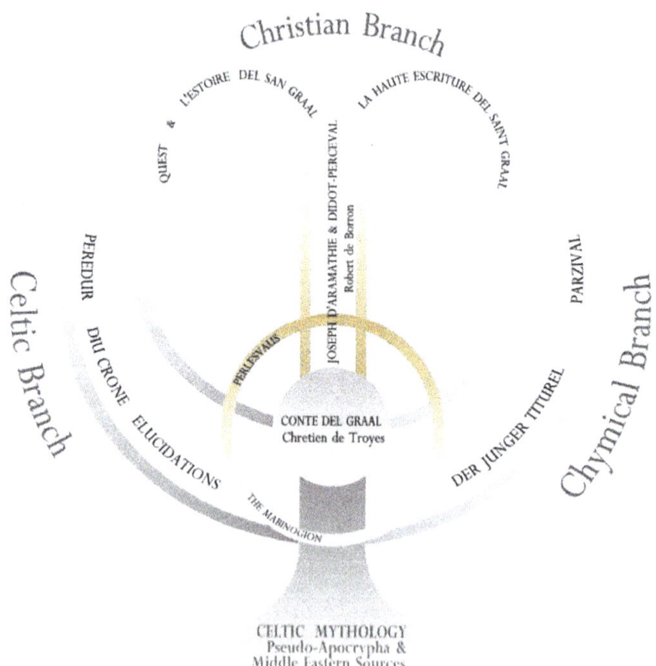
Christian Branch
QUEST & L'ESTOIRE DEL SAN GRAAL
LA HAUTE ESCRITURE DEL SAINT GRAAL
JOSEPH D'ARAMATHIE & DIDOT-PERCEVAL
Robert de Borron
PEREDUR
PARZIVAL
Celtic Branch
Chymical Branch
PERLESVAUS
DIU CRONE
ELUCIDATIONS
CONTE DEL GRAAL
Chretien de Troyes
DER JUNGER TITUREL
THE MABINOGION
CELTIC MYTHOLOGY
Pseudo-Apocrypha &
Middle Eastern Sources

A Three-fold Tree

Taken together, the Arthurian legends represent a most unusual convergence of three recognizable traditional worlds. Even though this characteristic is generally admitted it is rarely explored, at least in terms of all three, and so the implications of this convergence have been underestimated. As everyone knows, the Holy Grail is the cornerstone of Arthurian legendry, and in a recent book focusing on the Grail, a graphic representation of the presence of these three worlds has been attempted (opposite page).[1] This representation is given the form of a "Three-fold Tree:" While particular stories might represent branches, the three worlds themselves are rather obscurely identified at the roots of the tree as Celtic Mythology, "Pseudo-Apocrypha," and "Middle Eastern Sources." More simply, the roots of the Arthurian legends should be acknowledged as the tradition of the Celts, Christianity, and Islam.

---

[1] Malcolm Godwin, *The Holy Grail: Its Origins, Secrets & Meaning Revealed*, New York: Viking Penguin, 1994, page 15.

By the High Middle Ages, the era to which this literary manifestation principally belongs, what remained of the Celtic tradition had been subsumed by Christendom, and it is largely through the Arthurian legends that the memory of that ancient tradition has been preserved at all. As for Islam, its presence is rather awkwardly labelled "Chymical" in the above diagram, in order to emphasize Islamic Hermeticism of which alchemy (the "chymical") is but a particular application. The only work to properly explore the participation of Islam in Arthurian legend is Pierre Ponsoye's *L'Islam et le Graal*, and Ponsoye provides ample evidence of how this Hermetic influence proceeded more or less directly from Islamic esoterism, that is, from the very heart of that tradition and not from some philosophy transmitted from the ancient world.[2]

The branches of the above diagram illustrate that these Celtic, Christian, and Islamic elements are not present in equal measure within each story. In terms of the Grail stories, the earliest example belongs to Chrétien de Troyes' *Perceval* from around 1190, and so it is depicted at the trunk or core of the diagram. Wolfram von Eschenbach's *Parzival* followed in the early 13th century and is the most "Islamic" of the tales, and so it is the particular focus of Ponsoye's masterful study. The more explicitly Christian versions of the story appear more or less at the same time, while the Celtic influence is strongest in Welsh tales of Peredur that happen to appear later. Of course, for Medieval Christendom, the pre-

---

[2] Cf. Abd ar-Razzâq Yahyâ, *Le Maître de l'Or: Aperçus complémentaires sur la tradition hermétique*, Paris: Le Turban Noir, 2016.

Christian and the Islamic worlds were similarly "pagan." The author of *Parzival* traced the true story of the Grail to a "heathen" of Spain, Flegetanis; yet this name signals the influence of Islamic esoterism and the spiritual authority of Jesus, as Ponsoye has explained.

The figure of Arthur himself was known long before the time of Chrétien de Troyes. He is included among the historical kings of Britain in various annals, most importantly in that of Geoffrey of Monmouth; this source served to renew his renown some 50 years before Chrétien. Arthur had moreover been the hero of an ancient mythology, and his adventures included a raid on the Celtic underworld. In keeping with someone able to travel while still living upon the "paths of the dead," Arthur was believed by Medieval Britons to be ever-living, a notion first recorded by the Norman cleric Wace.[3] Chrétien who followed soon after likewise belonged to Norman society in France, but in his writings King Arthur becomes relegated to a position of overseer, and Arthur's court becomes the setting for adventures that become known as the "Matter of Britain." [4]

Chrétien introduced the world to the struggles of Lancelot as well as to the mystery of the Grail, though he left the story of the latter

---

[3] A comparable notion is found, for example, among the Modocs of Native California (see "The Modocs and a World's Heart" in *Guardians of the Heart: Essays on Sacred Geography*, Temple of Justice Books, 2022).

[4] It was because of their Norman aspect that J.R.R. Tolkien considered the Arthurian legends inadequate to serve as a "mythology for England" since the Normans were the conquerors of the English.

unfinished. It would seem that the name "Chrétien de Troyes," or "Christian of Tricassium," is a title or nom de plume that insists upon his attachment to the Christian world, no matter the themes in his works. Five poems are attributed to him, and as with the story of the Grail, each includes an account of an otherworldly marvel. With his poem *Yvain, or the Knight of the Lion,* there are valuable indications of how the Celtic, Christian and Islamic worlds are intertwined at the very core of the Arthurian legends.

The Rain Stone

In the story of the Knight of the Lion, the otherworldly marvel that Yvain must investigate involves a spring and an attendant power to conjure storms. Chrétien describes the setting for this marvel at the opening of his poem, which includes an evergreen tree, a bowl hanging from the tree for the spring water, and a special stone beside the spring. With the sprinkling of spring water upon the stone, a violent storm of wind and rain is the result, followed by sublime singing from birds in the tree. When Yvain causes such a storm, he is met by a champion whose role is to defend the land against the violence of this conjuration.

In a manner rather unusual in Arthurian studies, this marvel has been confidently identified with an actual spring in Brittany, the "British" region of France. Wace includes an account of this spring of Barenton in the forest of Broceliande in his *Roman de Rou*. Wace's relevance to Arthurian literature has already been mentioned, and his description is worth quoting not only to compare with Chrétien's, but moreover since it confirms that we are concerned here with an aspect of the Celtic tradition of the Bretons:

The fountain of Barenton
Emerges on one side near a large stone.
Hunters used to go
To Barenton in times of great heat,
And pour out the water on their bodies
And wet the stone on its upper side;
For this they used to have rain.
Thus it used to rain formerly
In the forest and roundabout,
But I do not know by what cause.
There one used to see fairies,
If the Bretons are telling us the truth,
And a number of other marvels…
But villains have devastated everything.
There I went seeking marvels,
I saw the forest and I saw the land;
Marvels I sought, but I didn't find them.[5]

Wace testifies here to the disenchantment of the spring of Barenton, no doubt a sign of the passing of the Celtic tradition. It is, of course, not necessary to assume that Chrétien is simply borrowing from Wace if we are dealing with a more widespread aspect of that tradition; after all, the Celtic veneration of springs is well attested.[6] It is therefore better not to ignore some interesting details found only in Chrétien's poem.

---

[5] 6395-6409.

[6] Cf. for especially relevant examples G.L. Hamilton, "Storm-making Springs, Rings of Invisibility and Protection. Studies on the Source of *Yvain* by Chrétien de Troyes," *Romantic Review II*, 1911.

The poet's description of the spring that "surges and seethes, though it's colder than marble"[7] suggests that he has a soda spring in mind. It is more particularly the stone, however, that seems especially unique. It is related at first that a Wild Man had "seen no other like it," and later that the stone, rather curiously, had "holes bored through, just like a wineskin."[8] This description necessarily recalls the ancient holed stones found throughout France, and indeed throughout the lands of the ancient Celts. While their traditional function eludes modern researchers, the best study of these "basin stones" in France admits the likely relationship between these stones and rain,[9] which accords with the writings of Wace and Chrétien. It is further worth considering that in Ireland where sacred springs are beyond numbering, a holed stone or bullaun[10] is often considered a sacred "well" in itself; even when a source of groundwater is absent, these stones still serve to hold rainwater.

We know a great deal more about the use of such stones from a traditional world that survived into more recent times than that of the ancient Celts. Remarkably, the holed stones of Native California are known precisely as "rain rocks." These sacred stones may still in some cases be found along the river systems of the California-Oregon borderlands, where there seems to be some variation in their

---

[7] 380-1. Quotations are from Barton Raffell's translation (*Yvain: The Knight of the Lion*, New Haven: Yale University Press, 1987).

[8] 424-5.

[9] Roger Mathieu, *Le Mystère des Pierres a Bassins*, Yssingeaux: Éditions Per Lous Chamis, 1984, page 113.

[10] The term "bullaun" is cognate with "bowl."

A holed stone in California

"The Holy Stone" of Dingle in Ireland
(below)

appearance and usage. In his study of the rain stones,[11] Robert F. Heizer describes them as pitted, which serves to account for the varied cup-marks upon their uppermost surfaces. Usually the smaller cups are called cupules, while larger holes are called "mortars," even when there is no evidence for their use as mortars. Academics presume the latter to be practical tools, but admit that the former must have a ritual significance since materialism offers no alternative explanation. The distinction is rather arbitrary, especially when both forms of cup-marks appear together upon the same stone; it seems preferable then to recognize a far subtler distinction.[12]

Heizer relates the experience of Roland Dixon in 1904, who in his study of the Shasta people searched for the "Gottville Rain Rock" along the Klamath River to no avail, even though it had previously been photographed. In 1948, however, during the construction of a highway along the river, the "missing" stone happened to be found, and was then further displaced to a regional museum. Apparently it had been buried, as Shasta informants explained, since the power of the stone could be activated only when uncovered. One informant recalled a time of drought: "So, my people pounded a large hole in the rock. Soon the rains came, and

---

[11] "Sacred Rain-Rocks of Northern California," California Indian Library Collections Project, 1989.

[12] There is a third type of cup-mark still rarer in California, much larger than the "mortars:" the so-called "Indian bathtubs," the dimensions of which are measured in feet rather than inches. Like the majority of "mortars," however, these appear in bedrock and should therefore be considered in a separate study.

there was a great flood. My people then buried the rock. It should have been left buried, for it is too powerful."[13] While this report indicates that the making of cups would bring rain, for the neighboring Hupa people, rain was conjured by simply sprinkling water upon a "rain rock" in an act of sympathetic magic,[14] which is precisely the method reported of the Celtic example. What is more, the memory of the Gottville stone's dangerous power would seem to provide another precise analogue with the cause of the violent storms in Chrétien's poem. It should therefore not be overlooked that in light of the California example, an interesting explanation presents itself for the disenchantment of the spring of Barenton: its "rain rock" has been lost, whether through "villainy" or deliberate burial, and the stone presently beside the fountain is just a stone.

Other comparisons between these Celtic and Native Californian examples are no less interesting. Wace reports that the Bretons had seen fairies at the spring of Barenton; Native tradition generally recognizes springs and other watery haunts to be the homes of such beings.[15] Further relating to matters

---

[13] Report documented by the Fort Jones Museum; the "Gottville Rain Rock" remains there far from the Klamath River (see "Stones of Exile," chapter 6 of *The Red and the White: Perspectives on America and the Primordial Tradition*, Temple of Justice Books, 2019).

[14] E. Breck Parkman, "Creating Thunder: The Western Rain-Making Process," *Journal of California and Great Basin Anthropology*, volume 15, number 1, Riverside: Malki Museum, 1993, page 93.

[15] See *American Elves* compiled by John Roth (Jefferson: McFarland, 1997), passim.

unseen, the cupped stones of Native tradition served as "gates to the supernatural world."[16] Ananda K. Coomaraswamy remains the finest expositor of these gateways in mythology worldwide and of the metaphysical principles involved, and in his important article "Symplegades," he examines the sequence of events that immediately follows Yvain's conjuring of the storm in Chrétien's poem.[17] Coomaraswamy explains that Yvain pursues the guardian of the spring into the Otherworld, and so we should admit that the stone at the spring is part of the gateway to Chrétien's supernatural world. Obviously, as Coomaraswamy reminds us, these motifs "are not the personal property of Chrétien," and he offers in his study that they belong instead to "a mythology of prehistoric and presumably Neolithic antiquity." In fact, specialists in the matter of the pitted boulders of America suppose that their use as "rain stones" began at least 7000-9000 years ago.[18]

In the Christian and Islamic worlds, the practice of praying for rain is well known, according to the shared example of the ever-living prophet Elijah; yet the memory of rain stones persisted. In his always rewarding *Christianity and Islam Under the Sultans,* F.W. Hasluck reports from the Ottoman Balkans the case of a "written stone" that was kept buried or else "it would never stop raining." Hasluck further observes:

---

16 Parkman, op. cit., page 97.

17 *Studies in Comparative Religion,* volume 7, number 1, Bedfont: Perennial Books, Winter 1973.

18 Parkman, op. cit., page 99.

> The idea of rain-making "written stones," it may be remarked, is familiar to the Turks, since Turk, their eponymous ancestor, is said to have received from his father Japhet (who, in turn, inherited it from Noah) a stone engraved with the name of God which had the property of causing and stopping rain. This particular stone has been lost, but stones are said to be sometimes found which possess the same properties and are supposed to have some vague connexion with the original stone of Noah.

What is more, the use of rain stones among Muslims has survived into modern times, albeit in a renewed form. In a study of the *yada* or "rain-producing stone" among the Turks, the author concludes her survey with a description of a contemporary rain ritual in Turkey: "the participants collected in 70, 700, 7000, or 70000 pebbles, read a verse for each from the Koran, placed the pebbles in bags, carried them to a river, and placed the bags in a river. They were supposed to stay there until the rain started and then taken out to stop the rain only if it rained too much."[19]

---

[19] Ilhan Basgöz, "*Yada*: A Rain-Producing Stone and the *Yada* Cult Among the Turks," *Journal of Popular Culture*, volume XVI, issue 1, summer 1982. The author continues: "The pebbles, of course, were the distant memory of the *yada* stone, and indicated their new function, which was the simple means of counting the number of verses that should be read from the Koran." This last statement is

Leaving aside the variety of methods, it should be emphasized that the Islamic tradition traces the use of rain stones to the prophet Noah and the beginning of the postdiluvian world. In *The Red and the White,* I associated the veneration of sacred stones with the renewal that followed the Flood of Native tradition. For the Hopi, whose lore has been preserved with notable detail, the beginning of the postdiluvian world involved the separation of Native people from their "white brother," with each keeping half of a broken tablet. If it is possible that this "brother" refers to a people of Europe – and this seems to have been the perspective of the Hopi - this lore suggests that the Celts received an inheritance comparable to that of Native America, with the shared tablet as its emblem.[20] Even without the testimony of the Hopi, it is clear enough that the shared use of rain stones should be attributed to a common source in the Primordial Tradition, since, to borrow the words of Ananda Coomaraswamy, "independent origins for such complex patterns are almost inconceivable."[21] As for the perpetuation of rain stones in the living tradition of Islam, this is in

---

disingenuous, however, since the stones are not simply for counting but also for bringing into contact with water, not completely unlike the sympathetic magic of the Hupa. The pitted boulders of America were not valued only for their geologic composition but rather for the marks upon them, and in the Muslim ritual, the Holy Qur'an transforms ordinary pebbles into very many sacred rain stones.

20 From this perspective, the early American search for the imaginary "Welsh Indians" was far from meaningless, since it signifies nothing less than the search for the representatives of the Primordial Tradition.

21 Op. cit.

perfect keeping with its identification with the Primordial Tradition itself.[22]

Nevertheless, it may be assumed that the use of the rain stone in Chrétien's poem did not proceed from an Islamic source, but from vestiges of the Celtic tradition. The same may not be maintained for the most essential characteristic of Yvain, however: his role as the "Knight of the Lion."

---

22 Cf. *The Red and the White* (op. cit.), page 60. Given that the influence of the Primordial Tradition is characterized by a "Hyperborean current," it is worth noting that the lore of the *yada* stone of the Turks belongs to Northern Eurasia.

The Lion of Allāh

It is often claimed that the Arabic language holds a thousand terms for the "king of beasts." Be that as it may, there can be no doubt that the lion naturally belongs to the Islamic world and is not native to Western Christendom. The great hero of the earliest days of Islamic history, Hamza the uncle of the Holy Prophet, was known as the "Lion of the Desert." In Medieval England, King Richard was known as "Lionheart," but this must fundamentally be attributed to Norman contacts with the East. After all, it is generally recognized that the Islamic lion served as an inspiration for Western European art and heraldry.[23] Admittedly the lion was already familiar to Western Europe through the Roman Empire, and the dominance of the Roman Church transmitted specifically Biblical lore about the lion. The appearance of the lion of *Yvain* in the 12th century, however, is rather lacking an obvious precedent, especially since in the Bible heroes like Samson - or even Daniel - are more often pitted against lions than identified with them.

---

[23] Michel Pastoureau, *Une Histoire symbolique du Moyen Âge occidental*, Paris: Seuil, 2004, page 53.

Academics have generally failed to appreciate the central function of the lion for Chrétien, despite his naming the poem the "Romance of the Knight of the Lion:"

> ...scholars who regard Yvain as a Celtic otherworld tale dressed up in French clothing, finding no close analog to the lion in Celtic lore, have paid little attention to him. And those who have concerned themselves with demonstrating that the source of the lion story was Latin or Greek have been interested more in the relation between Yvain's lion and that of Androcles (or some other one) than in his function in the poem. Those who have studied particularly the structure of the poem have attached more importance to the lion...[24]

Indeed, the lion is introduced at the precise center of the poem. Having fallen from his otherworldly attainment, Yvain comes upon the lion and a snake in combat and chooses to intervene against the poisonous serpent. Needless to say, a Medieval audience would not have failed to recognize in the combat of lion and snake a matter of symbolic significance.[25] At this pivotal moment, Chrétien

---

[24] Julian Harris, "The Rôle of the Lion in Chrétien de Troyes' *Yvain,*" *PMLA*, volume 64 number 5, Cambridge: Cambridge University Press, December 1949, page 1143.

[25] There is more to this symbolism, however, than the opposition of good and evil. In Oriental cosmology, the

provides a curious detail that should not be overlooked: "But because the snake had gripped the lion's tail in its poisonous teeth, he was forced to chop a piece from the tail, but he cut only as much as he had to, and he had no choice, there was no other way."[26] The attention placed upon the lion's tail (*keue* in Old French) is meaningful in the context of Yvain's conflict with Kay (*Keu*) of King Arthur's court, as a recent article has pointed out.[27] The author of this study does not dwell, however, on how this imagery relates to the matter of Chrétien's sources.

From at least the 11th century, leonine iconography in the Islamic world included a strange and recurring motif: the lion with a serpent-headed tail. Despite the obscurity of its significance, this iconography persisted for many centuries,[28] and we must suppose that Chrétien de Troyes is indicating an Islamic provenance for his lion by identifying its tail with the serpent's head. The identification is so close, in fact, that for the serpent to be eliminated the lion's tail had to be removed. Of course, for Christendom, and despite the Biblical injunction to

---

White Tiger of the West is positioned opposite the Blue Dragon of the East, and tiger and dragon are essentially equivalent to lion and serpent.

26 3381-7.

27 Lukas Hadrian Ovrom, "*Lion-Keu-Coupé*: A Missing Link in *Yvain* or *Le Chevalier au Lion*," *New Medieval Literatures 20*, edited by Robertson et al., Cambridge: D.S. Brewer, 2020.

28 For early examples and an attempt at interpretation, see Abbas Daneshvari, *Of Serpents and Dragons in Islamic Art: An Iconographical Study*, Costa Mesa: Mazda Publishers, 2011, pages 159-64.

be "wise as serpents," the snake or dragon has an overwhelmingly malevolent significance, and it is surely to indicate the purely benevolent character of Yvain's lion that the poet insists on removing all trace of malevolence from it. It should not be assumed, however, that the serpent's head upon the tail of the lion had the same meaning in the world of Islam, and it is far more likely that what was originally indicated by this iconography was a transcendent unity in which opposites are reconciled.

In any case, there is a very good reason why Chrétien de Troyes would position an Islamic lion at the center of his tale of chivalry. The inspiring role of Islamic chivalry in relation to medieval Europe has been recognized at least since 1849 thanks to von Hammer-Purgstall's "Sur la chevalerie des arabes antérieure à celle de l'Europe, et sur l'influence de la première sur la seconde;"[29] after all, paths of chivalry were not established at the origins of Christianity, whereas the Prophet of Islam is reported to have said, "Every prophet has a vocation, and my vocation is knightly striving." If the lion is of central significance for the tale of *Yvain*, the same may in fact be maintained for the traditions of Islamic chivalry or *futuwwah*. The chivalric example of `Ali bin Abi Talib, who became known as the "pivot" of *futuwwah*,[30] was from the rise of Islam paramount,

---

[29] *Journal Asiatique*, 4th series, volume 13, pages 5-14. The title equates European chivalry with that of Christians, whereas Islamic chivalry was, of course, very much at home in the Iberian peninsula.

[30] Husayn Wā`īz Kāshifī Sabzawārī, *The Royal Book of Spiritual Chivalry (Futūwat nāmah-yi sultānī)*, Chicago: Kazi, 2000, page 4.

and he came to be exclusively identified with the lion.[31] All initiatory chains of knighthood in Islam were traced to him, and so anyone who received the tied belt or sash of investiture would become, in a sense, a "knight of the lion."

Yvain's path to redemption begins from the pivotal moment of the tale, and Chrétien describes the relationship of knight and lion upon this path as that of "companions." This relationship further demonstrates nothing other than the essence of *futuwwah*: to love God and his creatures more than oneself.[32] In his study of the lion's function, Julian Harris emphasizes that the tale of *Yvain* is far more pious than Chrétien's other works: "it is the romance of the purposeful knight who, with the help of God - and the lion - was able to overcome all sorts and descriptions of men, giants, and devils - i.e., vices." Concerning the devils specifically, who "could not be overcome by human skill, human strength, and human implements" but who are nevertheless conquered by the lion, Harris poses the crucial question: "if this is the case, can the lion be regarded as anything else than a symbol of God?"[33] The lion of Yvain is more precisely the emblem of `Ali, who is known traditionally as *Asādullāh al-ghālib*, the "Victorious Lion of Allāh."

---

[31] This identification is rooted in the name *Haydar* that was bestowed upon him by his mother (cf. Gibril Fouad Haddad, *The Rightly-Guided Caliphs*, ISCA, 2023). The use of leonine imagery to identify him can be traced at least as far as the Fatimids of Egypt.
[32] Cf. Michel Chodkiewicz' introduction to *The Book of Sufi Chivalry* (New York: Inner Traditions, 1983).
[33] Op. cit., page 1163 and 1160.

`Ali with the lion
from an Ottoman *Siyer-i Nebi* (above)

Lion with a serpent tail[34]

---

[34] From Thierry Zarcone, "The Lion of Ali in Anatolia: History, Symbolism and Iconology," *The Art and Material Culture of Iranian Shi'ism. Iconography and Religious Devotion in Shi'i Islam*, edited by Pedram Khosronejad, London: I.B. Tauris, 2012, page 110.

There is another place where the lion oversees a convergence of Arthurian chivalry with Islam, and this place was the last stronghold of Islamic rule in Spain before its conquest. This stronghold is the palace of the Alhambra in the city of Grenada, and the words *Lā ghālib illa Allāh* ("there is no victory except in Allāh") repeat throughout its decorative plan. At the heart of the Alhambra is the Court of Lions, called *al-Riyād as-Sa`īd* in Islamic sources, where a circle of twelve stone lions supports the basin of its fountain. Alongside this courtyard is the Hall of Justice or "of the Kings," where a collection of paintings of mysterious provenance and even more mysterious iconography adorn its ceiling. On display are knightly themes from a world inhabited by Christians and Muslims, but it was only recently that Jerrilynn Dodds demonstrated that the iconography relates most closely to Arthurian legendry.[35] However, the depictions do not clearly correspond to specific stories, and so Dodds maintained that the 14th century painters did not understand their source material. Other academics have sought to revise her interpretation, suggesting other sources to account for the lack of clarity, but all seem to agree that the Arthurian legend of Tristan is a principal subject.[36]

Given that the Arthurian legends hold a fusion of elements from the Celtic, Christian, and

---

[35] Jerrilynn D. Dodds, "Paintings in the Hall of Justice in the Alhambra: iconography and iconology, *The Art Bulletin*, volume 61, June 1979.

[36] Cf. Cynthia Robinson, "Arthur in the Alhambra? Narrative and Nasrid Courtly Self-Fashioning in the Hall of Justice Ceiling Paintings," *Medieval Encounters*, volume 14, numbers 2-3, Leiden: Brill, 2008.

Islamic worlds, the stories surrounding Sir Tristan are especially exemplary in this regard. Its Celtic foundations are indicated by the stories' many analogues found as far as Ireland, while Islam is explicitly represented by the Muslim knight of the Round Table, Sir Palamedes. According to the Christian account, Sir Tristan must defeat Palamedes in a tournament for the hand of Iseult; upon the ceiling of the Hall of Justice, however, it is rather a Muslim knight who is shown defeating a Christian, which has compelled at least one scholar to accuse the painters of enviously altering their source material. Of course, since not all the imagery in the paintings corresponds to a single known source, these figures needn't be Tristan and Palamedes specifically. Now, Chrétien de Troyes has not been cited among the most likely sources for the iconography of the paintings, yet we may discern within the ceiling's chivalric landscape a Wild Man, fountains, trees teeming with birds, and even a pacified lion, and these motifs could easily have been inspired from the story of *Yvain*. It may be that the immediate source of the iconography is lost to us, yet it is also possible that the paintings are themselves a unique story in images in which the Islamic element happens to be dominant.

The most repeated motif in the ceiling paintings of the Hall of Justice are lions and lion heads, which is suitable for imagery comprehensible both to Christian and Islamic chivalry. Most significantly, the central panel of the ceilings includes lion supporters of heraldic emblems belonging to a specific chivalric order, the Order of the Band, an order founded by King Alfonso XI of Castile in 1332. Its distinctive mark of a "band" or

The emblem of the Order of the Band in the Alhambra

sash recalls the girding of Islamic chivalry,[37] and so it is fitting that Muslim rulers and perhaps knights were supposedly admitted into the order. It has been argued that these emblems were added to the Hall of Justice after the fall of Grenada as a sign of Christian conquest,[38] but this loses sight of the fact that the Order of the Band did serve to unite Christians and Muslims with a shared bond of chivalry, albeit briefly. There had been, of course, conditions during the Taifa periods of Medieval Spain when Muslim and Christian forces were compelled to forge alliances, but the inclusion of

---

37 On the role of Islam in the development of Christian chivalry along the Christian-Muslim frontiers, see Ponsoye, op. cit.

38 Ana Echevarria, "Painting Politics in the Alhambra" (ibid.). The emblem depicted is known as the "Royal Bend of Castile," and would continue to be used apart from the chivalric order in heraldic formulations of Spanish political power. Curiously, dragon heads hold the band (above) in a manner recalling the serpent heads that were attached to the tails of lions; and as we have seen, these heads could have alternatively a benevolent or malevolent significance.

Muslims within the Order of the Band rather recalls the example mentioned above of Sir Palamedes and the Round Table of King Arthur. The depiction of the emblems of the Order upon the ceiling of the Hall of Justice with its Arthurian themes suggests that this characteristic shared between the real and imaginary orders of knighthood was understood.

It may seem strange to discover tales of Arthurian chivalry in southern Spain, but not if the meeting of Christian and Islamic traditions is recognized as being integral to their formulation. Even so, it should not be forgotten that Chrétien de Troyes and the Normans were really "Northmen," like the Visigoths of Spain, but that it was nevertheless the Celtic rather than the Norse tradition that served as the ancient foundation of the Arthurian stories. In fact the story of *Yvain* seems even to have been transmitted to the extreme northern land of Iceland, as the evidence on the carved church door of Valþjófsstaður demonstrates (opposite page).

Clearly the branches of the Arthurian Threefold Tree extended over the full extent of Europe. Yet the fertile ground for this tree was a pivotal landscape forever associated with the Celtic tradition, and it is for this reason that Arthurian legendry is still remembered as the "Matter of Britain."

Hölzerne Kirchenthüre aus Island. (Im Museum zu Kopenhagen.)

Custodians of the Grail

The Table of Jesus and his Companions
from a Persian edition of the *Qisas al-Anbiya,* c. 1580

The Three Tables

After Chrétien de Troyes introduced the world to the story of the Grail, and left it unfinished, many Arthurian stories may be considered more or less direct continuations of his tale. Like distinct fruits attached to the diverging branches of our Three-fold Tree, three forms of the Grail after Chrétien become identifiable emblems of the traditional worlds participating in the tree's generation. For Chrétien, the Grail is a wide golden dish or bowl, which is what the word signifies in old languages of southern Europe: "a cup or bowl of earth, wood, or metal."[39] For Wolfram von Eschenbach who most clearly represents the Islamic contribution, the Grail is a stone from Paradise, and so immediately recalls the focus of Muslim veneration, the Black Stone of the Temple in Mecca.[40]

---

39 Friedrich Diez, *An etymological dictionary of the Romance languages*, Williams and Norgate, 1864, p. 236.
40 Besides Ponsoye, op. cit., cf. John Matthews, *The Grail: Quest for the Eternal*, London: Thames and Hudson, 1981, page 90. According to the doctrines of *futuwwah,* the Black Stone holds the names of those called to it, while the names

As should be expected, however, the Christian form of the Grail becomes best known; beginning with the writings of Robert de Boron, the Grail cup is a relic from the life of Jesus.

In the most Celtic of the tales, the Welsh tale of *Peredur,* it is not a dish that is the focus of attention but the severed head that it contains. This head belongs to the uncle of Peredur, just as the uncle of Perceval is the wounded Fisher King of other versions that followed Chrétien's with his "Rich Fisher." For the Celts, the importance of the symbolism of the head is well attested, as in the stories of Bran the Blessed, for example; yet Ananda K. Coomaraswamy has brought attention to a tale from Hindustan "of a very archaic type" that he considers to be a variant of the Grail legend, and in this tale the head is likewise of principal importance and belongs to the father of the hero.[41] Coomaraswamy summarizes the tale of Prince Mahbub in his survey of the mysterious saint who in this instance oversees the revival of the prince's father, and who is "guardian and genius of vegetation and of the Water of Life." The power of this saint who is known as al-Khidr, the "Green Man," corresponds with the description of the Grail by Wolfram von Eschenbach: "Such power does the stone give a man that flesh and bones are at once

---

of those called to Wolfram's Grail appear upon its surface; see my introduction to Kāshifī, op. cit.

[41] "Khwājā Khadir and the Fountain of Life, in the Tradition of Persian and Mughal Art," *Ars Islamica,* volume I number 1, Ann Arbor, University of Michigan Press, 1934.

made young again."[42] It is therefore worth recalling that according to Islamic esoterism, al-Khidr belongs to an elite rank of immortal saints to which Jesus also belongs; and if all three versions of the Grail seem strangely bound to this saintly rank, the connections are only reinforced by the presence of a "Fisher," for the fish is the emblem of Jesus among Christians and of al-Khidr among Muslims (see page 84).

Of course, symbolism is a universal language, with sacred roots that remain above historical developments; it can therefore be difficult to trace the distinct influences that contributed to the development of the Matter of Britain. Sometimes the authors themselves provide indications that are helpful in this regard, as in the well-known example of Wolfram von Eschenbach's attribution of his account to a source beyond Christendom. Yet even in the most singularly Christian of the Arthurian tales there is a suggestion of distinct influences, with the history of the Grail presented in distinct stages that number exactly three.

In the so-called Vulgate Cycle of the 13th century, wherein the character of Galahad is introduced as the perfect example of monastic knighthood, the Holy Grail is related to a succession of three sacred fellowships, and specifically to their "tables."[43] First there was "the table of Jesus Christ, where the apostles broke bread on many occasions." Second there was the table of the Holy Grail,

---

[42] Wolfram von Eschenbach, *Parzival*, translated by Mustard and Passage, New York: Vintage Books, 1961, page 252.

[43] The following summary includes quotations from P.M. Matarasso's translation of *The Quest of the Holy Grail* (Baltimore: Penguin Books, 1970, pages 97-9).

instituted "in memory and in likeness of the first…in the days of Joseph of Arimathea when the Christian faith was first brought to this land." While "this land" means Britain, it is very specifically Glastonbury in Somerset that comes to be identified in British legend as the place where Christianity was first brought. The account of this second table includes a miraculous feeding of "four thousand and more" by the power of the Grail from only twelve loaves of bread, as well as a description of the "Seat of Dread" that becomes better known as the "Siege Perilous." In this history, the punishment attached to the Seat of Dread is reserved for the rival who challenges the true inheritor of Saint Joseph of Arimathea.

Third in the succession of tables was the Round Table, "devised by Merlin to embody a very subtle meaning," and the author elaborates on its significance:

> For in its name it mirrors the roundness of the earth, the concentric spheres of the planets and of the elements in the firmament; and in these heavenly spheres we see the stars and many things besides; whence it follows that the Round Table is a true epitome of the universe. For from every land, be it Christian or heathen, where chivalry resides, knights are seen flocking to the Round Table…When Merlin had established the Round Table, he announced that the secrets of the

> Holy Grail, which in his time was covert and withdrawn, would be revealed by knights of that same fellowship.

It would seem to be straightforward enough to regard each of the sacred tables as emblematic of each of the three traditions participating in the Matter of Britain. The first table would naturally correspond to the Christian tradition and the second table to the Celtic tradition of Britain that received it, while the third table would relate to Islam in some measure simply by including "heathen" knights such as Sir Palamedes. In actuality, this simplistic set of correspondences relies on a superficial understanding of the tables. The truth of the matter is far subtler and demands a more careful consideration of the precursors to the Round Table.

A Holy Thorn of Glastonbury

Heavenly Signs on Earth

The description here of the "table of Jesus Christ" is strange. Of course, already we have with Robert de Boron the identification of the Holy Grail with the cup used by Jesus at the Last Supper, and the account of the second table, that of Joseph of Arimathea, does include the motif of the "Seat of Dread" that is a clear reference to the Last Supper. However, in accounts of that singular event the table is given no importance, and here the table of Jesus Christ is described as being used "on many occasions." The second table is also the setting of a miracle that is clearly in the likeness of events in the Gospels, both the feeding of five thousand on five loaves of bread and two fish that is reported in all four Gospels, and the feeding of four thousand on two fish and seven loaves of bread reported in the Gospels of Matthew and Mark.[44] Even though the former report is the only miracle of Jesus agreed upon by all four Gospels, a table of Jesus Christ does not figure in any of these reports. There is, however,

[44] Perhaps the twelve loaves of the Holy Grail are meant to combine the five loaves and seven loaves of both Gospel accounts.

a clear precedent for such a table, though it does not belong to Christendom. In the Holy Qur'an of Islam, the chapter (*surah*) called "The Table (*al-Ma'idah*)" concerns a table of Jesus Christ specifically; and given the participation of the Islamic tradition in the Matter of Britain, we must consider this source that has surprisingly been overlooked.

> 112. *When the disciples said: O Jesus, son of Mary! Is thy Lord able to send down for us a table spread with food from heaven? He said: Observe your duty to Allah, if ye are true believers.*
> 113. *(They said:) We wish to eat thereof, that we may satisfy our hearts and know that thou hast spoken truth to us, and that thereof we may be witnesses.*
> 114. *Jesus, son of Mary, said: O Allah, Lord of us! Send down for us a table spread with food from heaven, that it may be a feast for us, for the first of us and for the last of us, and a sign from Thee. Give us sustenance, for Thou art the Best of Sustainers.*
> 115. *Allah said: Lo! I send it down for you. And whoso disbelieveth of you afterward, him surely will I punish with a punishment wherewith I have not punished any of (My) creatures.*

Even though the petition was made and accepted, commentators insist upon Jesus' unease with his disciples' request. The otherworldly table descended and returned daily to the heavens for a number of days – "on many occasions" - and this miracle became a test of faith. Now, it is worth insisting that the table's descent and return is in perfect keeping with Medieval descriptions of the Grail, specifically with Wolfram's description of its heavenly origin, and with the Vulgate Cycle's insistence upon its being raised to heaven with the passing of Galahad. As for the form of this miracle, Karima Sperling explains that the meaning conveyed by the word *al-ma'idah* "is not a physical table with four legs, but rather the feast laid out on it…The idea of a meal presented as a whole, laid out on top of a table or tray is the image intended."[45] With "tray" we are not far from Chrétien de Troyes' original vision of the Grail as a wide golden dish, and at the very least, the insistence upon the setting of a feast for the Grail appears to be precise. Moreover, the fish that commentators describe as the centerpiece of Jesus' table is certainly echoed by the Fisher of the Grail castle. The traditional commentary also includes the motif of the healing of the sick at this table,[46] which may not be surprising

---

[45] Karima Sperling, *The Family of `Imran: Mary, Jesus, Zachariah, and John*, Little Bird Press, 2020, page 209. Sperling includes a curious description of how angels descended with the table upside down, and reversed its position upon reaching the earth (page 211); the imagery of these two positions for the receptacle, alternatively heavenly and earthly, recalls the symbolism of the two hemispheres that form a circle (see Sperling, *Following Moses: The Story of Joshua*, Little Bird Press, 2022, page 148; as it relates to Jesus, cf. chapter 8 of my *Paths of the Western Sun* volume II, *The Nine Sisters of California*, Temple of Justice Books, 2023).

[46] On the fish and the healing of the sick, see ibid., page 211.

in the context of a miracle of Jesus, but is admittedly inseparable from the qualities of the Grail.[47]

Above all, however, the unusual "*punishment*" associated with the table of Jesus in the Holy Qur'an may not be without relevance for the supernaturally wounded king in the Grail legends. Muslim commentators describe the hoarding of provision from the table as the cause for a terrible punishment, and is it possible that a Grail container had been separated from the table in an act of hoarding and passed on as a relic? Obviously this idea belongs to the imagination, but so too does so much of the Matter of Britain. The expression "*for the first of us and for the last of us*" would seem to include the Last Supper, and so the specific failure of Judas; yet the phrase "*last of us*" may relate more generally to the continued and deeply confused presence of the Holy Grail in the consciousness of Western culture after the end of Christendom. In a very real sense, the wounded king of Arthurian lore and the accompanying wasteland pertains to a failure of faith amidst prosperity,[48] and in that regard the Western world suffers still.

Be that as it may, if the first among the three tables may be understood to relate to the Christian as well as the Islamic tradition, it is clear enough that the second table is synonymous with the

---

[47] Recall Wolfram's renewal of "flesh and bone;" and while Wolfram insists on the form of the Grail as a stone from heaven, it includes the power to "give sustenance."

[48] Cf. ibid. for the wounding of the Grail king who inappropriately fought for love by the "heathen" who fought for the Grail (page 256); in keeping with this interpretation, the Muslim has faith in the heavenly table by virtue of the Holy Qur'an.

establishment of the Christian tradition in Britain. The landscape of Glastonbury in England still retains the memory of that establishment at a number of hallowed places. Saint Joseph of Arimathea is held to have planted his staff on Wearyall Hill upon his arrival, and the Glastonbury Thorn long grew there as testament to the miraculous flowering of his staff; a number of its descendants are still to be found in the town.[49] The ruined site of Glastonbury Abbey preserves the location of Saint Joseph's original settlement. Most notably in the present context, the sacred spring below Chalice Hill is associated with the Holy Grail, and its redness supposedly signifies the presence of the Grail (the "Chalice") hidden in the hill.[50]

As part of his researches into the ancient secrets of Glastonbury,[51] John Michell explored the sacred geometry of Saint Joseph's settlement. I have addressed elsewhere Michell's role in discovering Glastonbury Tor's position upon a ley line dedicated to Saint Michael, but even with this dedication, the evidence he revealed certainly predates the establishment of Christianity. His discovery

---

[49] Its proper descendants have the wondrous characteristic of blossoming twice a year, including, significantly enough, at Christmas. British royal custom includes having a Glastonbury Thorn branch decorate the monarch's table at the Christmas feast.

[50] Of course, the redness here is linked to the blood of Jesus that was allegedly collected in the chalice by Saint Joseph, and this link depends upon the deliberate conflation of the Grail with the sacrament of church doctrine.

[51] Michell focused attention on Glastonbury with *The View Over Atlantis* and continued to do so intermittently throughout his *oeuvre*.

followed that of Katharine Maltwood, who in the 1930s brought to light the most iconic and controversial element of Glastonbury's ancient past, an arrangement of huge zodiacal effigies upon the wider landscape. René Guénon confirmed the legitimacy of her discovery in his article on "The Land of the Sun," basing his judgment upon certain traditional details of the arrangement.[52] For example, he draws attention to the effigy of Aquarius:

> In the Glastonbury Zodiac, the sign of Aquarius is represented in a rather unexpected way by a bird in which the author rightly thinks she recognizes the Phoenix, and which is carrying an object that is none other than the "cup of immortality," that is, the Grail itself...Moreover, according to Arab tradition, the *Rukh* or Phoenix never alights on land anywhere other than on the mountain *Qāf,* which is the polar mountain; and in the Hindu and Persian traditions *soma* comes from this same "polar mountain" (also designated by other names), that *soma* which is identical with *amrita*

---

[52] This article may be found in the collection *Symbols of Sacred Science* (Hillsdale: Sophia Perennis, 2004); it bears repeating here that Michell cites Guénon precisely on the subject of the Grail (see for example *Twelve-Tribe Nations and the Science of Enchanting the Landscape,* London: Thames and Hudson, 1991).

A view of Glastonbury Tor from Chalice Hill

> or "ambrosia," the draught or food of immortality.[53]

Guénon does not dwell upon another remarkable fact, that in an arrangement covering miles of the Somerset landscape, the sign of this cupbearer should be positioned precisely over Chalice Hill and the legendary location of the Holy Grail. Glastonbury Tor is also encompassed by the effigy, and so the commanding hill takes on greater significance in light of Guénon's commentary; we are also reminded that the name "Arimathea" is

---

53 "The Land of the Sun," op. cit. Recall that the phoenix figures in Grail lore: "By the power of that stone the phoenix burns to ashes, but the ashes give him life again" (Wolfram von Eschenbach, op. cit., page 251).

uncannily similar to the word *amrita.* As far as the spring water is concerned, the very meaning of the name "*phoenix*" relates to the color red. All this demonstrates how the second table of Joseph of Arimathea represents a harmonious meeting of the Christian and Celtic traditions in a land that mirrored the heavens.

Unfortunately, there have been very recent developments in Glastonbury that threaten, at least superficially, that harmony. On the opposite side of Wellhouse Lane from the Chalice Well another spring rises that is called the "White Spring" on account of its Calcite deposits. The close proximity of the two springs suggests they belong to the same complex, even if the White Spring is associated with Glastonbury Tor rather than Chalice Hill. Regardless, no lore of importance seems to have been attached to these waters that lack the redness of Chalice Well. In the 19th century the spring was dug out and a utilitarian wellhouse was built to provide a reservoir for the water supply, though the mineral content of the White Spring made maintenance difficult. In time the building was sold, and in the 21st century its excavated grotto was converted into a so-called "temple." Now, during the course of the 20th century the gardens surrounding Chalice Well had been set aside in order for visitors to enjoy the sanctity of the site while respecting all faiths. This contrasts starkly with the Neopagan focus of the White Spring, where statues based on Celtic motifs have been set up to receive the veneration of visitors, and photography is not allowed in order to respect a single faith. While the Chalice Well testifies to the survival of ancient wisdom into Christian times, the grotto of the White Spring accommodates an anti-

Christian rival.[54] Fortunately, both spring waters remain freely accessible on either side of Wellhouse Lane between the hills.

In his evaluation of the zodiacal effigies, René Guénon makes an important observation: "If these figures have been preserved in such a way as to be still recognizable today, it is presumably because the monks of Glastonbury carefully maintained them until the Reformation, which implies that they must have retained the knowledge of the tradition inherited from their distant predecessors, the Druids, and no doubt from still others before them." In other words, even if the upheaval of the Reformation meant that the very existence of the Zodiac would have to be rediscovered, this example demonstrates how an authentic memory of the Celtic tradition was perpetuated within Christian esoterism rather than through some imaginary pagan authority. There is more: Guénon adds an intriguing footnote here on the Templars as "Guardians of the Grail:" "the establishments of the Templars frequently seem to have been situated in the neighborhood of megalithic monuments and other prehistoric ruins,

---

[54] Along with the springs there is the example of the so-called "Egg Stones." In my study of Glastonbury's importance (chapter 7 of *Sacred Geography and the Paths of the Sun*, Temple of Justice Books, 2021), I had occasion to mention the original stone described by Frederick Bligh Bond in 1913 and located within the grounds of the Abbey; somehow a rival egg stone has come to be venerated on Glastonbury Tor, and its position on the hill is opposite and out of sight of the Abbey. This rival stone lacks the special marks distinguishing the true Egg Stone, the Omphalos of Glastonbury.

which we should perhaps regard as more than a mere coincidence."[55] The custodians of the Grail were called "Templars" by Wolfram von Eschenbach, which no doubt resonated with the order's well-known affinity for the tradition of Islam; but if the Order of the Knights Templar also preserved an ancient understanding of the European landscape as Guénon suspects, then all three of the traditional influences at work in the Matter of Britain - Celtic, Christian, and Islamic - must be brought together by those who are truly to be regarded as Guardians of the Grail.

The presence in modern times of the Islamic tradition in Glastonbury has reunited these three elements, at least virtually. Representatives of Islamic *tasawwauf* or Sufism are the subject of "From Celts to Kaaba: Sufism in Glastonbury" by Ian K.B. Draper.[56] The author observes that the most prominent Haqqani Sufis seemed "to associate themselves with the Christian traditions of Glastonbury" while dissociating from the pagan; but as we have seen with the example of the White Spring, it is rather the pagan element that has

---

[55] Op. cit. The example of Saint Indracht at Glastonbury suggests Christian awareness of the mystery of the Saint Michael ley line; see my *Sacred Geography and the Paths of the Sun* (op. cit.). As far as the Templar Order is concerned, we would do well to compare the number of its founding knights - 9 - with the archetypal presence of this number in the names of megalithic monuments (see *The Nine Sisters of California*, op. cit., chapter 2).

[56] *Sufism in Europe and North America*, Abingdon: Routledge, 2004, chapter 8. On the Haqqani Order in Glastonbury, cf. also *Sacred Geography and the Paths of the Sun*, op. cit.

deliberately separated from Glastonbury's traditions to invent their own. Indeed, Draper adds that the Haqqaniyya more especially was "engaging with the whole quasi-Christian discourse of a Celtic church," that is, with a Christian tradition that preserved the memory of ancient Britain. Draper describes a gathering of the Haqqani Sufis at the Chalice Well Gardens, and remarkably compares another of their meetings with the "feeding of the five thousand" that should be recognized as recalling the Holy Grail, given the evidence mentioned above. Another development is certainly worth mentioning that came after Draper's study: when she passed away, the unofficial leader of the Haqqani Sufis in Glastonbury, Zahra ("Zero") Quensel, was buried outside the town, but the location chosen happens to coincide with the very center of the Glastonbury Zodiac.

The existence of the zodiacal circle upon the landscape where Saint Joseph of Arimathea is believed to have established the second table of the Grail is remarkable indeed, given the meaning of the third table devised by Merlin. It will be recalled that the Round Table mirrored in its roundness "the stars and many things besides," and so there is a direct link between the legendary location of the second table and the form perpetuated by the third table. Maltwood's *A Guide to Glastonbury's Temple of the Stars* speculated on the relationship between the Matter of Britain and the effigies, but Guénon disputed its interpretation of the Grail legends as dramatizations of the landscape zodiac. Even so, a symbolic correspondence is undeniable, as for example in the numbering of the Knights of the Round Table at twelve like the zodiacal houses. The identity of the table's designer is no doubt significant here, since there is no clearer personification of an inheritance from the Celtic tradition than the "Druid" Merlin. The third table therefore references the Celtic tradition as well as the "heathen" Islamic, as we have seen, while the Christian Grail is described as "withdrawn." Each of the three tables may therefore be understood to correspond not to each of the three traditions involved in the Matter of Britain, but rather to a unique convergence of two of these traditions in turn. Again, the first table involves both the Islamic and the Christian, the second table the Christian and Celtic, and the third table the Celtic and Islamic.

There is a Medieval artistic motif that serves to demonstrate these three convergences, as it were, though its original significance is obscure. This motif goes by various names, including the "Three Hares," and became widespread especially in the churches of Devon (below) just to the southwest of Somerset. The motif is also known as the "Tinners' Rabbits" owing to an association with the tin miners of this region, and these miners also happen to be connected in local legend with Saint Joseph of

Roof boss in Throwleigh Church, Devon

Arimathea. In any case, the design involves a visual puzzle, since only three ears are depicted, yet each of the three rabbits are shown with two ears. If the three ears may be understood to represent the Celtic, Christian, and Islamic elements, each rabbit's pair of ears demonstrates the composition of each of the three tables of the Grail legend.

The use of this symbol for our purposes is not so completely arbitrary as it seems. At the center of the design is the form of a triangle, and since the design is rotational, this triangle may be presented as on the opposite page in an inverted position. As René Guénon has indicated, the inverted triangle serves to represent the heart as receptacle, as it did in ancient Egypt, and so also the receptacle of the Grail.[57] Just as the story of the Grail has been formed by Celtic, Christian, and Islamic elements, so is this triangle formed by the three ears that serve to represent these elements in this design. Of course, we should not assume that this meaning was in a deliberate manner attached to the Three Hares in the Middle Ages, yet there is a very good reason why this design should not be consequently dismissed. There is clear evidence that this motif entered England through the Islamic world, since it may be traced through Persian examples all the way to a Chinese origin. For this reason, it provides independent testimony of the participation of the Islamic influence upon the spiritual landscape of traditional Britain.

57 "The Sacred Heart and the Legend of the Holy Grail," *Symbols of Sacred Science*, op. cit.

Illustration 7 CALENDÉRY *VOYAGEUR.* 11

The Green Turk

The Three Hares motif has been traced specifically to the Buddhist cave complexes of Dunhuang in western China, but we should not therefore imagine that Buddhists were in any way responsible for transmitting this motif to Britain. While the examples in Dunhuang have been dated to the 7th and 8th centuries, the westward distribution of this motif seems to postdate these compositions by some 500 years. By the time of this distribution, Buddhist expansion westwards had ceased, overwhelmed by the eastward expansion of Islam; and more importantly, representatives of Islamic esoterism had established themselves in Buddhist cave complexes. A specific example is provided by the Qalandars and the cave shrine known as Yiti Kalandar, or the Seven Qalandars, in the region of Turfan. The term *qalandar* is rather mysterious with an unknown etymology,[58] but here Seven Qalandars

---

[58] John Subhan in *Sufism: Its Saints and Shrines* (Lucknow: Lucknow Publishers House, 1938, page 309) relates that the word "is derived from one of the names of God in Syriac," by which is meant the primordial "solar language (*lughat suryani*)" of Adam. On the complex connotations of

refers to a group of saints known to Christendom as the Seven Sleepers, and who are called in the Holy Qur'an the Companions of the Cave;[59] in the latter they are also called *fityan* or "knights," and it is perhaps in this sense that the word *qalandar* serves as a synonym. Certainly in Islam the way of chivalry (*futuwwah*) and of the Qalandar alike involve heroic self-negation. The title of Qalandar was specifically used in the Islamic world for a particular spiritual type that involved wandering as a spiritual practice.

The Qalandars were long recognized by a distinctive dress and shaven appearance, and their influence upon Sufi orders such as that of the Bektashi is undeniable; but the organizing of this spiritual type within the orthodoxy of the orders is traced to India and to a saint known as Shah Khizr Rumi Khapradari. It is not without significance that this saint's supernatural longevity recalls the hagiography of the Companions of the Cave. In the Holy Qur'an, the deathless sleep of the Companions is calculated at 309 years.[60] The span of Shah Khizr Rumi's life is supposed to have been some 250 years,

---

the term in the Islamic world, see chapter 6 of *Mysteries of Dune* (Temple of Justice Books, 2020).

[59] It is worth observing here that the shrines dedicated to the Seven Sleepers in the Islamic and Christian worlds are legion, and in some cases the same shrine may be venerated by representatives of both traditions concurrently, as at the shrine in Jordan. A deliberate attempt to extend this practice into lands belonging to the descendants of the Celts is embodied in a unique example in Brittany, where the orientalist Louis Massignon organized an annual pilgrimage in the 20th century for Muslims as well as Christians to a shrine that incorporates a megalithic dolmen.

[60] XVIII, 25.

between 1107 and 1349. Even this claim, however, is far exceeded by the legendary lifespan of his master, `Abdul-`Aziz al-Makki, who is traditionally regarded as a Companion of the Holy Prophet Muhammad himself. An overview of his legendary life appears in *A History of Sufism in India*:

> At his request the Prophet allowed him to lead a retired life in a mountain cave and the Prophet Muhammad himself prayed for his welfare and longevity. Shaikh `Abdu'l-`Aziz reappeared from the cave when `Ali bin Abi Talib was Caliph and after swearing allegiance to him, the Sheikh reverted to his hermit's life in a cave. He reappeared in the third century Hijri and became the disciple of Bayazid Bastami. Once more he retired to the solitude of the forests, emerging after two hundred years to initiate Khizr Rumi. Shaikh `Abdu'l-`Aziz then went to Ajodhan, and like Imam Mahdi...disappeared into a grotto (*sardabad*) on the outskirts of the town. Before his final disappearance he prophesied he would reappear at the same time as the last Imam Mahdi before the Day of Resurrection.[61]

The lifespan of Shah Khizr Rumi Khapradari happens to coincide with the era of the Grail legends

---

[61] Saiyid Athar Abbas Rizvi, *A History of Sufism in India*, volume I, New Delhi: Munshiram Manoharlal Publishers, 1997, page 304.

in Europe, and this coincidence demands our attention because of the meaning of his title: "Khapradari is connected with a cup which he called Khaprā, and always carried with him. It is said that the cup possessed the miraculous quality of being able to supply to any one whatever was wanted."[62] It is well known that this attribute is associated with the Celtic antecedents of the Grail;[63] and it should not be overlooked that Khizr Rumi is also the namesake of al-Khidr,[64] the Green Man mentioned earlier whose power was likewise associated with Wolfram von Eschenbach's description of the Grail.

From Wolfram comes another description that is worth comparing to Shah Khizr's longevity and his possession of a miraculous cup: "There never was a human so ill but that, if he one day sees that stone, he cannot die within the week that follows."[65] Curiously, the successors to this saint in India were also endowed with seemingly supernatural longevity. According to the order's hagiography, the

---

[62] Subhan, op. cit., page 311.

[63] Cf. Matarasso's introduction to *The Quest of the Holy Grail* (op. cit.), page 13.

[64] "Khizr" is the Persian form of "Khidr."

[65] Op. cit., page 252. It is not known what material the Khaprā was fashioned of. Wolfram insists more on the Grail's stone composition than on its shape; these characteristics happen to be reconciled in the wondrous stone bowl of the Buddha. I mentioned this relic of the Buddha along with Wolfram's Grail in *Mysteries of Dune* (op. cit.), where I further offered that the similarities between them may derive from their common association with the celestial sphere of Mercury; given the importance of the Grail to the Matter of Britain, it is worth recalling the observation of Julius Caesar that the ancient people of Britain venerated Mercury above all others.

immediate successor to Shah Khizr was Sayyid Najmuddin Ghawth ad-Dahar Qalandar, who passed away in 1432 at the age of 200. Sayyid Najmuddin's successor was Qutb ad-Din Qalandar Sarandaz-i-Ghawthi, who passed away in 1518 at the age of 145, and he was "the last of the Qalandari saints to have lived to over 100 years."[66] For this reason, these three saints should be regarded to comprise a singular "category" among the Qalandars, a category led by Shah Khizr Rumi, the possessor of the miraculous cup; their shared longevity is thus not easily dissociated from the possibility that this cup possessed other Grail-like attributes, and served as an heirloom. Unfortunately, there seems to be no record of the fate of this cup after Shah Khizr Rumi Khapradari; still, it is worth observing that while Chrétien's first story of the Grail belonged to the lifetime of Shah Khizr, the "final" Grail story of the Middle Ages, *Le Morte d'Arthur* by Sir Thomas Malory, belonged to the lifetime of Qutb ad-Din.

There are, however, further details in the hagiography of these three saints which are far more suggestive concerning our subject. Significantly enough, Sayyid Najmuddin is supposed to have twice visited England and China. At the very least, his itinerary demonstrates that the transmission of the Three Hares motif that originated in China and ended up in England might be easily accomplished, even by an individual. As for the third in this succession of saints, the import of Qutb ad-Din Qalandar's title must be considered, given the importance of Shah Khizr's: "The title *Sarandāz*

[66] Subhan, op. cit., page 312.

means one who casts away his head, and is said to have been given to him because at the time of performing Dhikr his head would become severed from his neck." We have mentioned the role of the head in the most Celtic of the Grail legends, and Guénon has indicated a relationship between the cup and the dome,[67] which in the human form corresponds to the head. What is more, the Sanskrit term *khappar*, no doubt the source of the name Khaprā, means both cup and skull. To fully confront the implications of the title *Sarandāz* for the Matter of Britain, however, we must reevaluate one of the best-known stories of Camelot, *Sir Gawain and the Green Knight*.

This poem from the late 14th century is too familiar to require a detailed summary here, and it should easily be recalled that its principal theme is the "beheading challenge." In his article "Sir Gawain and the Green Knight: Indra and Numaci,"[68] Ananda K. Coomaraswamy demonstrated "the cosmological principle at stake: we are witnessing the drama of World Creation where the Primordial One, the Supreme Person (*Purusha*) has voluntarily to be dismembered through a Sacrifice *in divinis* so that a predestined portion of Infinity's fathomless bounty may be released for manifestation by this beheading, this diremption of Heaven and Earth."[69] Given the primordiality of this sacrifice, we should not be at all

---

67 "The Symbolism of the Dome," *Symbols of Sacred Science*, op. cit.

68 *Speculum: A Journal of Medieval Studies*, University of Chicago Press, January 1944.

69 Whitall Perry, "The Dragon that Swallowed St. George," *Studies in Comparative Religion*, op. cit., volume 10, number 3, Summer 1976.

surprised that this theme should be found in many traditional forms, including, apparently, the Celtic tradition.[70] What concerns us here, however, is that there seems to be no obvious predecessor in Celtic lore for the man called the Green Knight. Instead, this figure all in green has naturally recalled for some the immortal al-Khidr, literally "The Green," especially since the Green Knight survives his beheading.[71] This survival happens to be in perfect keeping with the hagiography of Saint George, the name by which al-Khidr is known by Christians. However, the Islamic associations of this green man must have been clear enough by the 15th century for a retelling to be called *The Turke and Sir Gawain*.

Given the foregoing, we must now relate the Islamic resonance of the Green Knight specifically to the namesake of al-Khidr, Shah Khizr Rumi Khapradari, or rather to the category of Qalandar saints associated with him. The title Rumi refers to East Rome, and therefore Anatolia. By the 15th century and the composition of *The Turke and Sir Gawain,* Anatolia had become the land of the Turks, at least according to the Christian understanding.[72] Regarding the attributes of the Green Knight, I have elsewhere observed that the axe was of special

---

[70] Derek Bryce, *The Mystical Way and the Arthurian Quest,* Lampeter: LLanerch Enterprises, 1986, pages 122 ff.

[71] Cf. Perry, op. cit., as well as Bryce, ibid., and my introduction to *The Royal Book of Spiritual Chivalry* (op. cit.).

[72] For the Ottomans who were the inheritors of the Romans, the name "Turk" was rather derogatory, suggesting something like "hillbilly," whereas "Ottoman" means the "People of Othman" and carried no ethnic connotation.

Original depiction of the Green Knight

significance within Sufism. Of course, the axe may simply be seen as the instrument necessary to the "beheading challenge," but it should not be ignored that within Sufism the axe served especially as an emblem of the Qalandars and their self-negation.[73] The strange home of the Green Knight, the so-called Green Chapel, no doubt recalls the Celtic tradition, since it is described as a "barrow;" yet it may also be compared with the *sardabad* that is the dwelling place of `Abul-`Aziz al-Makki, the first of the Qalandars. The meaning of *sardabad* is both "grotto," as we have seen, but also "small mound,"[74] and both these characteristics belong also to the description of the Green Chapel. As for the beheading motif itself, it clearly belongs to a primordial formulation, but there is no denying that the role of the Sarandaz, the "one who casts away his head," belongs at the same time to the spiritual legacy of Shah Khizr.

At the conclusion of "Sir Gawain and the Green Knight," the motto of England's Most Noble Order of the Garter is mysteriously invoked. The composition of the poem in the late 14th century followed the Order of the Garter's official founding in 1348, and so the anonymous poet would seem to be offering some sort of commentary on the order. Certainly a garter features in the poem, whereas the history of the order lacks a convincing account of the emblem's origin. Recently it has been claimed that its

---

[73] I mention the significance of the axe in my introduction to *The Royal Book of Spiritual Chivalry* (op. cit.); for an example of the axe serving as a distinctive emblem of the Qalandar, see Thierry Zarcone, "The Sword of `Alî (Zülfikar) in Alevism and Bektashism," *Journal of the History of Sufism* 6, 2015., page 116.

[74] Subhan, op. cit., page 310.

inspiration is in the Spanish Order of the Band and its ceremonial girding, and this only confirms the participation of Islam in its foundations.[75] Even if this connection to Islam is at best indirect, al-Khidr remains the bridge between the Green Knight and the patron saint of the Order of the Garter, Saint George. And what of the motto itself? In Old French, the motto is *Honi soit qui mal y pense*, meaning "Shamed be whoever thinks ill of it," which presumes the disapproval of public opinion. The matter of public opinion is likewise inseparable from the way of the Qalandars; indeed, a classical definition goes so far as to observe that "the *qalandarī* seeks to destroy accepted custom."[76]

Still, it is by no means clear why an order of chivalry to which a society's leaders belong could be at odds with social norms, even if in the present day there are many who think ill of it. The solution may very well depend upon some sort of initiatory attachment between the Order of the Garter and the order of the Qalandars;[77] this attachment would

---

[75] Rogers, Clifford J., "The symbolic meaning of Edward III's Garter badge," *Military Communities in Late Medieval England: Essays in Honour of Andrew Ayton*, edited by Baker, Gary P et al., Woodbridge: Boydell, 2018. Cf. the section "The Lion of Allāh" above.

[76] Shihāb ad-Dīn Suhrawardī quoted in "Sufis, Malamatis, and Qalandaris," Appendix B of Trimingham's *The Sufi Orders in Islam* (Oxford: Oxford University Press, 1971). This definition could easily be applied to the Green Knight's disruption of the court of King Arthur at the beginning of the poem.

[77] Idries Shah in his popular book *The Sufis* (New York: Doubleday, 1964) mentions Shah Khizr in this very context, though he calls him "Sayed Khidr" and fails to appreciate his significance to the Matter of Britain.

seem to be demonstrated by *Sir Gawain and the Green Knight.* Acknowledging this attachment does not help us detail a history of the Qalandars in Britain, of course. Not until 1914 and the founding of the Sufi Order of Hazrat Inayat Khan is Sufism officially established in London, and this post-colonial development would seem to have nothing to do with the Matter of Britain. Still, it is certainly worth noting that its Indian founder belonged to the spiritual lineage of the Qalandars, and that its followers would also eventually find their way to Glastonbury.[78]

As we have seen, it is possible to discern throughout the Matter of Britain signature traces of the spiritual legacy belonging to the Qalandars of Shah Khizr. Even more remarkably, at the present time there are signs of this legacy resurfacing in an unprecedented manner, and it is to this development that we must turn.

---

[78] See Draper, op. cit.

The Green Man King

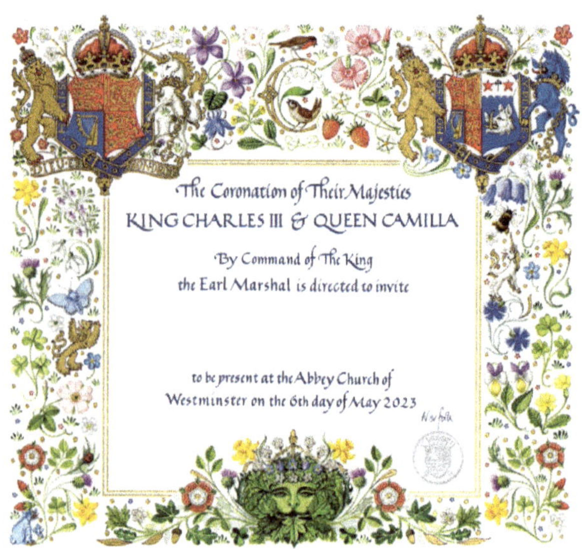
The Coronation of Their Majesties
KING CHARLES III & QUEEN CAMILLA
By Command of The King
the Earl Marshal is directed to invite
to be present at the Abbey Church of
Westminster on the 6th day of May 2023
Norfolk

The Invitation

In anticipation of the coronation of HM King Charles III, I presented a collection of essays that among other things addressed the luminous aspect of the symbolism of the dragon. In the western world, this aspect is most familiar from the Arthurian milieu, since King Arthur has always been associated with the title "Pendragon" that was first borne by his father Uther. The significance of this title belongs principally to an astral context, and in the first of the collected essays, I offered an interpretation of some of the astronomical events that coincided with the accession of the new king.[79] Of course, with the patron saint of England being Saint George, the darker side of dracontine symbolism is even better known in Britain, and it is worth pointing out that the tenebrous aspect of the dragon is not absent from astronomy either. We have in mind here the iconography of the lunar nodes, for these have traditionally been identified with a dragon that threatens to "swallow" the

[79] "Celestial Events Accompanying the Accession of HM King Charles II," *Pendragon: Essays Collected for the Coronation of King Charles III*, Temple of Justice Books, 2023.

celestial luminaries during eclipses.[80] Very remarkably, there was a penumbral lunar eclipse on the eve before the coronation; and just as day is the complement of night, the day following this eclipse was reserved for the celebration of the luminous "Pendragon King."

These astronomical events not only served as a reminder of the supramundane character of symbols, but also demonstrated the fullness of its language.[81] In "The Arcane Setting for the Coronation" I addressed some of the meanings attached to the ceremony's traditional elements, and no doubt the media coverage of the King's coronation offered an unprecedented opportunity to appreciate these elements. Without digressing into a detailed review of a ceremony in which the mundane often played a principal role, it is important now to consider other significant elements that appeared specifically with the crowning of this king. After all, as a patron of the arts and indeed an artist himself, HM King Charles III consciously served as the subject of a royal "art" that drew the attention of the world, even if the world fell short of fully comprehending it.

This incomprehension surely cannot be blamed on the event itself, given the iconography adorning the formal invitation issued in advance of the coronation (see page 70). The choice of the central emblem for the design was in distinct contrast from invitations accompanying previous coronations; that

---

[80] See *The Nine Sisters of California,* chapter 2.

[81] Obviously modern people have proven incapable of understanding this language in its fullness, with the pentagram and the swastika, for example, becoming recognized exclusively in their darker aspects.

of HM The King's immediate predecessor, for example, gave the crown jewels with Saint Edward's Crown this position, as might be expected for the occasion. Instead, the emblem chosen for King Charles III was a mysterious face, and even though the imagery was uniquely designed for the event, there was no doubt that this visage was meant to recall the so-called "green men" adorning Medieval British churches. A statement from Buckingham Palace accompanied the release of the invitation:

> The invitation for the Coronation has been designed by Andrew Jamieson, a heraldic artist and manuscript illuminator whose work is inspired by the chivalric themes of Arthurian legend…Central to the design is the motif of the Green Man, an ancient figure from British folklore, symbolic of spring and rebirth, to celebrate the new reign.

Despite this official clarification, the presence of the Green Man immediately generated considerable controversy. Popular opinion assumed the motif to be pre-Christian, a notion seemingly supported by the Palace's use of the word "ancient."[82] In 1939 this notion was put forth in an article appearing in the journal *Folklore* by Julia Somerset, better known as Lady Raglan, who is

---

[82] This assumption was expressed, for example, on social media by Winston Marshall, an evangelical Christian and former member of the band Mumford and Sons, who characterized the motif as "paganism" and falsely accused HM The King of violating the "first commandment."

considered to have coined the name "Green Man." Subsequent scholarship has largely dismissed her theory of the motif representing the survival of pagan belief, even while Neopaganism has put her theory into practice. It is worth pointing out, however, that the earliest definitive evidence for the Green Man motif in Britain is found in Norman churches of southern England, that is, not in a pagan setting but in the same milieu as the design of the Three Hares. Curiously, the two motifs are often found together.

Another opinion sought to explain the Green Man of the King's coronation as essentially Christian. In a letter to *The Guardian*, Stephen Miller advertised a position he takes up in a recent book[83] that the motif refers specifically to the legendary Quest of Seth. This widespread legend focuses on an errand undertaken by the son of Adam for oil from Paradise with which his father might be healed. In Christian versions, Adam is hoping to be saved from death, but Seth is refused entry into Paradise; and instead of the "Oil of Mercy," he is given three seeds from the Tree of Knowledge that he is told to place in the mouth of his father upon his passing.[84] The seeds subsequently grow from the grave of Adam into trees that ultimately become the "True Cross" of the Crucifixion. Despite the mouth of Adam being

---

83 *The Green Man in Medieval England: Christian Shoots from Pagan Roots*, Cambridge Scholars Publishing, 2022.

84 In the Islamic version, Seth is given Paradisal olives and oil on Mount Sinai, and his father is healed. On the subject of the history of the Grail, René Guénon refers to a source he does not cite that involves Seth successfully returning to Paradise to retrieve the sacred cup (*The King of the World*, op. cit.).

the receptacle for the seeds, and the fact that many (but not all) images of the Green Man involve leaves sprouting from his mouth (and not a grave), there is little else that Miller can offer to prove his theory. Direct associations with Adam or the True Cross[85] (or even the trunks of trees) are lacking from the iconography of the Green Man, and the latter's often menacing aspect is not an attribute of Adam. For this reason, it is more reasonable to make a connection with the Green Knight of Arthurian legend,[86] as is very often done; and besides, the Green Man imagery specifically concerns a living head that is likewise the central motif of the beheading challenge.

Given the connections between the Green Knight and al-Khidr, then, we must acknowledge that the choice of the Green Man for the occasion on 6 May is not merely coincidental, since 6 May is Hidrellez, the festival of al-Khidr.[87] These signs only confirm the King's knowledge of the Green Man's identity in Islam. Somehow, however, this fact was ignored by the so-called experts consulted by the

---

[85] It should be noted, however, that the True Cross was nevertheless involved in the coronation of King Charles III. The coronation procession was led by the Cross of Wales, a reliquary that His Majesty literally had a hand in crafting, and this reliquary holds two shards of the True Cross that were a personal gift from Pope Francis to mark the occasion. The Cross of Wales is so named because it has been given by the King to the Church of Wales, and by holding shards of the True Cross it replaces the lost Cross of Neith of the Princes of Gwynedd.

[86] Before his work for the invitation, Andrew Jamieson had already composed a depiction of the Green Knight.

[87] Cf. *Pendragon*, op. cit.

media when the invitation controversy was being addressed. As a result, while the contribution of Lady Raglan was being disparaged, no one was able to concede that her choice of the title "Green Man" serves as a perfectly suitable translation of the name "al-Khidr." Along with the inherent Islamic significance that is clear enough, the designer of the invitation has chosen to include explicit references to the Celtic and Christian worlds. The Green Man is crowned both by the acorn of the oak as well as the blossoms of the thorn. Obviously the oak tree is a quintessentially Celtic emblem, with even the name "Druid" etymologically relating to "oak." As for the thorn, there can be no doubt that its blossoms signify the Glastonbury Thorn. Among vegetal emblems, it is the Holy Thorn above all that represents Christianity in Britain through the presence of Saint Joseph of Arimathea.[88] We have, then, in this artwork by Andrew Jamieson a conjunction of Celtic, Christian, and Islamic meanings, a conjunction that, as we have seen, is in perfect keeping with the "chivalric themes of Arthurian legend."

---

88 Since the "crown of thorns" is a familiar Christian motif, it serves here as a reminder of the bond between the Green Man and Jesus according to Islamic esoterism.

Face of the Time

If Arthurian legendry provided a glimpse of the Green Man in the form of the Green Knight, there are much clearer traces of al-Khidr to be gleaned from the Medieval hagiographies of Islamic esoterism. Such records belong to myth and spirituality rather than conventional history, and it is indeed futile to restrict this figure to a single temporal context; after all, as I mentioned above, al-Khidr appears in Islam as an immortal and so beyond the restrictions of time.

The revelation of the Holy Qur'an presents al-Khidr in the pre-Islamic period in the company of Moses. Remarkably, al-Khidr is presented as a guide for the great prophet, and traditional commentaries attribute this relationship to the superior knowledge of al-Khidr that derives directly from the Divine Presence. With a boat, a youth, and a wall, al-Khidr takes actions based upon his knowledge of events not yet come to pass: the approaching army's use of the boat, the youth's future tyranny, and the threat to an inheritance within the wall.[89] In each case al-Khidr directs the course of future events, and this

---

[89] XVIII, especially 71-82.

only confirms his position above the shifting courses of time. Moses fails to understand the choices of his guide, however, and though the latter explains his actions, he does so only after announcing his parting from Moses.

In the same chapter, the surah of the Cave (*al-kahf*), the Holy Qur'an relates the story of Dhul-Qarnayn immediately after the meeting of Moses and al-Khidr. Commentators identify Dhul-Qarnayn with Alexander the Great, and so it is not without significance that al-Khidr also appears in traditional histories as a companion of the great conqueror. In particular, al-Khidr joins Alexander's quest for the Water of Life, a quest that is also known from Christian sources. Al-Khidr succeeds in the quest while the conqueror could not, and so immortality is assigned to the one and mortality to the other, and it is worth emphasizing that this is due to the fact that al-Khidr and Alexander the Great had parted ways. This parting may therefore be compared with the parting of Moses and al-Khidr.

There is another important comparison to be made. According to Islamic esoterism, the planetary sphere of Jupiter is under the authority of Moses. From the astrological perspective shared by many traditions, Jupiter pertains especially to royal or temporal power, in keeping with the role of Jupiter/Zeus as the king of the Classical pantheon; and obviously Alexander the Great embodies a fullness of temporal power. For the Greek world, Alexander was even known as the son of Zeus. In relation both to Moses and Alexander, then, al-Khidr serves as the superior authority, and while it may be admitted that spiritual authority must always be regarded as superior to temporal power, al-Khidr demonstrates an authority specifically confounding to a perspective limited by time. Even the tracing of al-Khidr's immortality to the quest of Alexander the Great fails to account for his appearance in the earlier era of Moses.[90]

To understand how these considerations relate to the peculiar iconography of the Green Man, we must first acknowledge that there are variations in the foliate faces of Medieval England. Lions and dragons with foliage sprouting from their mouths also appear in stonework, and so these faces cannot be ignored in the iconographic study of the Green Man.[91] Since they too can be menacing or malefic they present the same ambiguous character. We mentioned above the association of the Green Man with the Three Hares motif that has been traced as far as China. In looking for a possible prototype of this iconography, allowance should therefore be made for possibilities far removed from Europe.

In fact, such a prototype may be found in China once again, where it is called the "Taotie," although its Indian analogues are clear, and its use even extends to Mesoamerica. The symbolism of the monstrous Taotie long precedes the name applied to it, which literally means "glutton." In India the face

---

[90] It is often observed that both Moses and Alexander the Great are depicted with horns in works of art, and while the title Dhul-Qarnayn relates to this characteristic, the following observation by René Guénon should be recalled: "The word *qarn* has another meaning as well, that of 'age' or 'cycle' and, most commonly, 'century'" ("The Symbolism of Horns," Symbols of Sacred Science, Hillsdale: Sophia Perennis, 2004).

[91] Cf. Jeremy Harte, *The Green Man*, Andover: Pitkin, 2001, pages 12-3.

is that of a lion or dragon, but in René Guénon's short article on the subject, he insists that the Taotie does not depict any animal in particular but rather a devouring monster. This "monster," however, has far more than a malefic significance:

> ...what is involved is a symbol of the "Supreme Identity" absorbing and sending forth the "Light of the World" in turn...Coomaraswamy has thus rightly said that this face, whatever its various appearances, is truly the "Face of God" that both "kills and makes alive."[92]

Guénon further observes that this symbolism specifically relates to Time "as 'destroyer,' or rather 'transformer.'" These aspects all belong to the formulation of the Green Man, whose monstrous mouth sends forth signs of life. Time brings the springtime after winter,[93] and rebirth must be

---

92 "Kāla-mukha," *Symbols of Sacred Scie*nce, op. cit. On `Ali, the Lion of Allāh, and the Supreme Identity, see "The Place of Ivan Aguéli" in *Guardians of the Heart*, op. cit. These two aspects of the Supreme Identity are clearly indicated in the various emblems of `Ali, including the lion with the serpent's tail discussed earlier as well as his bifurcated sword; `Ali's role as "gateway" to the City of Knowledge relates directly to Guénon's reference to the "Door of Deliverance" and "Jaws of Death." It is also worth noting in this connection that the customary phrase recited after the mention of `Ali's name means "May Allāh ennoble his face," no doubt for the sake of the one reciting.

93 More exactly, this iconography relates to the winter solstice as the *janua coeli* and the rebirth of the Sun; see "Kāla-mukha," op. cit.

preceded by death. The story of Sir Gawain takes place at the renewing of the yearly cycle, and the Green Knight arrives in Camelot holding an axe in one hand and a bough of holly in the other. To regard the face of the Green Man only in terms of fertility is unbalanced, whereas balance is always a characteristic of its composition.

Nevertheless, there is no doubt that Buckingham Palace was correct to associate the Green Man with the verdure of spring. According to the Prophet of Islam, "Khidr was so named because he sat on a barren white land once, after which it turned luxuriantly green with vegetation."[94] In harmony with its timing upon the spring festival of Hidrellez, the Coronation demonstrated that the Green Man was more than a decoration for the invitation alone. The headpieces worn by the royal princesses, for example, were understood to be "a nod to a motif used throughout Charles' coronation of the Green Man."[95] Instead of green, however, it was clear that blue was the color chosen for the proceedings; yet blue is the color of the Order of the Garter, the order that is under the patronage of al-Khidr, and Garter robes and badges were worn openly.

---

[94] *Sahih Bukhari*, "Book of Prophets."

[95] Elise Taylor, "The Hidden Meaning Behind Princess Charlotte and Princess Kate's Matching Silver Flower Crowns," *Vogue*, 6 May 2023. It should also be noted that in other commissioned works tied to the Coronation, Andrew Jamieson included in each case the face of the Green Man, and while there is some variation in the depictions, the crown of oak and thorn is invariably present.

In Islamic esoterism, al-Khidr is considered a "hidden" saint, that is, he remains anonymous to the majority of believers; after all, even Moses was not able to keep company with him for long. For this reason, manners (*adab*) require that the initiate treat every stranger "as if they are al-Khidr." It is therefore worth acknowledging the presence of a stranger in Westminster Abbey on 6 May that happened to attract the attention of the media. A cloaked and hooded figure with a long staff was glimpsed on security camera passing beneath the quire screen prior to the Coronation ceremony, and the figure's movement across the orientation of the church and method of holding the staff seemed strange indeed. Initial reports dubbed the anonymous figure the "Grim Reaper," despite the lack of an obvious reason (like a scythe). Enough public attention was focused on the figure, however, for a formal explanation to be offered by the Abbey, which amounted to little more than conjecture. It was claimed that the hooded figure was most likely an unknown "verger," a lay assistant in Anglican church services. Vergers, however, are not usually hooded and instead wear distinctive hats. Regardless, what makes this strange appearance so compelling is that the mysterious figure appeared immediately below the arch of the quire screen where the best-known image of the Green Man in Westminster is on display (see top of page 85), though it remained hidden from the camera on the other side of the screen.

In considering the possible presence of the Green Man, then, it is not without meaning that observers were reminded of the "Grim Reaper" rather than one who "makes alive;" and while experts debated whether the Green Man is pagan or Christian, no one recognized the mysterious figure in profile (see bottom of page 85) as a veiled reference to the traditional Islamic icons of al-Khidr such as the one on the following page.[96] Even if we restrict our view to the face of the Green Man, the present relevance of its symbolism for the world is clear enough, given the pervasive signs of an imminent apocalypse that necessarily involves death as well as life.[97]

---

[96] Even Westminster's proposed identification suggests the symbolism of the Green Man, since "verger" derives from a word for "branch."

[97] Cf. *The Nine Sisters of California*, chapter 8.

British rule in India succeeded that of the Mughals who recognized an "investiture by al-Khidr" for representatives of the Imperial power

The Steward

Beyond the vocation of temporal ruler, there are more specific ways in which HM King Charles III is related to Moses and Alexander, companions of al-Khidr. As I have noted elsewhere, King Charles III is the son of HRH Prince Philip who was born on the Greek island of Corfu, and so HM The King is a "son of Philip" as was Alexander the Great. The degree to which the King may be compared with Moses depends upon a cautious consideration of British Israelism, and this would take us too far from our subject. What rather warrants our attention is the curious manner in which the new king was identified with the Green Man himself instead of these companions. This seems to have been made explicit first with the October 2022 of *The Critic* magazine which featured a rendering of the newly acceded king with a crown of foliage.

Of course, this ruler's allegiance to the vegetable kingdom has long been recognized if not respected; decades ago he was mocked in the media for speaking to plants. Following the release of the invitation, however, Charles was openly hailed as "the Green Man King."[98] Now, *shah* is an Islamic term for "king," and even if the title "Green Man King" is not widely used, it was prefigured in the name of Shah Khizr, the saint whose spiritual legacy imprinted Arthurian England long ago. A Green Man King is, in truth, his namesake.

We have seen that this legacy involves themes of beheading and of perennial life, and so it must be observed that in choosing to be called Charles III, His Majesty is attached to these same themes within his own royal heritage, specifically through the Stuart dynasty. The Stuart king Charles I was, of course, martyred by means of decapitation in 1649, which demonstrated the only interregnal period in British history. The monarchy was revived in 1660 with the martyred king's son, and so the reign of King Charles II became known as the Restoration; in a real sense, however, the monarchy itself did not suffer death, since King Charles II was officially declared to have been the rightful king upon the death of his father. Very significantly, given the hagiography of Saint George who is repeatedly martyred and returned to life, the coronation of King Charles II took place on Saint George's Day, 23 April 1661. Crown jewels lost to the interregnum were replaced for this event, including a new version of Saint Edwards' Crown, and these were in turn used for the coronation of King Charles III.

Unique to the latter's coronation was the specific design of the Anointing Screen (opposite), and this design more than anything else relates to

[98] This phrase was used particularly in articles by Aris Roussinos.

the specific identity of the new king. The screen served to hide the monarch during the anointing, but at the same time its design presented witnesses with an opportunity to reflect upon the personal reality of the ruler. Upon the screen, the cypher of HM King Charles III is depicted upon the trunk of a great tree, the leaves of which hold the names of the 56 countries of the Commonwealth. The trunk of a tree is a symbol of the axis of the world (*axis mundi*), and HM The King is here identified with it. What is more, the consecrated oil for the anointing itself was sourced largely from olive trees growing on the Mount of Olives in Jerusalem, the burial place of HM The King's paternal grandmother, Princess Alice of Battenberg. The anointing therefore testified to HM

The King's unique bond with Jerusalem, the traditional "center of the world."[99]

If a tree may serve as an emblem of King Charles III, it is worth recognizing that this is more than a "speculative" association. His example over many years planting countless trees demonstrates an "operative" connection, in keeping with his efforts to restore environmental balance in Britain and indeed for the entire planet. In the last years of his mother's reign, the former prince and HM Elizabeth II planted the first tree in Windsor Great Park for a project called "The Queen's Green Canopy." The project served to commemorate the Queen's Platinum Jubilee, though it continued after her passing for another planting season until a reported 3 million trees had been planted in Her Majesty's name. At the end of the 2023 season, HM King Charles and his heir, HRH The Prince of Wales, planted a tree together at Sandringham House. Along with its inherent value, the planting of these trees demonstrated a specialty that HM Elizabeth II had highlighted for her House of Windsor in 2021: "the leading role my husband played in encouraging people to protect our fragile planet, lives on through the work of our eldest son Charles and his eldest son William."[100]

Likewise in 2021 and just before the launch of The Queen's Green Canopy, Prince Charles planted a tree in Oxford's Botanic Garden to mark 400 years since its founding in the time of the Stuarts. Alongside the young tree a plaque has been placed

---

[99] Cf. the "Blessed Tree" of the Holy Qur'an, "*an olive neither of the East nor of the West, whose oil would almost glow forth (by itself) though no fire touched it* (XXIV, 35)."

[100] "The Queen's Speech at the COP26 Evening Reception."

that includes an important indication: "This tree was raised from seed of the original *Pinus nigra* that grew here from c1830-2014 and was much loved by JRR Tolkien." The profound regard that Tolkien the Oxford don had for all trees is well-known from his writings: "In all my works I take the part of trees as against all their enemies."[101] The renewal of this tree in Oxford might specifically be compared with an example of central importance to Tolkien's *The Lord of the Rings*, the hallowed White Tree that is withered and dry until the return of the king. In *Alchemy in Middle-earth*, I maintained that the "restoration of the White Tree is of course emblematic of the healing of the Grail kingdom."[102] The young tree in the Botanic Garden, however, is black (*nigra*) and not white; and in my commentary of Tolkien's Great Work, I specifically compare the former Prince of Wales not to King Elessar but to his representative the rightful Steward of Gondor. Now with his choice of name, HM King Charles III succeeds Charles I and Charles II of the Stuarts, and "Stuart" is of course the same as "Steward."

There is obviously a tree more emblematic of the Grail kingdom, as we have seen: the Glastonbury Thorn. During the English Civil War, shortly after the arrest of King Charles I, the sacred thorn upon Glastonbury's Wearyall Hill was cut down by the king's enemies. Descendants of the original tree believed to have been planted miraculously by Saint Joseph of Arimathea survived in the town, however, and it was with the

---

[101] Letter to the *Daily Telegraph*, dated 30 June 1972.

[102] Page 68; Tolkien himself suggested that its renewal meant that "'The worship of God would be renewed, and His Name be again more often heard (page 102).'"

Restoration of Charles II that the royal custom of bringing a cutting to the monarch's table at Christmastime reportedly begins. Eventually a thorn was replanted on Wearyall Hill, but in 2010 this tree was violently desecrated, and the date chosen for the attack seemed deliberately timed to prevent the royal cutting's selection. Another direct descendant of the Holy Thorn was replanted on the site, but it too suffered from vandalism and was ultimately removed in 2019.

Even more recently in 2023, a great sycamore tree along Hadrian's Wall was cut down at a place known as Sycamore Gap due to its long presence there, though the tree itself was better known popularly as the "Robin Hood Tree" after being featured in a 1991 film. It is generally accepted that Robin Hood is more mythological than historical and somehow related to the Green Man. In all likelihood, it is the Islamic dimension of the Green Man that mysteriously accounts for the regular inclusion of a Muslim amongst his companions in recent versions of the myth.[103] In fact, Robin Hood's only companion in the film at the Sycamore Gap tree is the Muslim, who even prays there along Hadrian's Wall. Remarkably, Robin Hood's role in the scene is to assert ownership of the tree and prevent its being felled. Nevertheless the Robin Hood Tree has now been felled, or to prefer Tolkien's choice of word, "murdered," and Hadrian's Wall even suffered some damage.

A short walk along the wall from Sycamore Gap is a place known as Sewingshields, and this place is among those in Britain where King Arthur

---

[103] Cf. *Sacred Geography and the Paths of the Sun*, page 114.

and his knights are supernaturally hidden, at least according to local legend. Such places represent a specifically British version of sites dedicated to the Seven Sleepers,[104] the "Knights" or "Companions of the Cave" who were mentioned above in connection with the Qalandars. Given their number throughout the Christian and Islamic worlds, the importance of these places is less in their historical claims to authenticity than in their testifying to a future "awakening" or appearance of the hidden saintly hierarchy. Each place therefore has a special relationship with the Unseen. The story of the Companions of the Cave is related in the surah of the Cave, that is, in the same surah in which the stories of al-Khidr and Dhul-Qarnayn are told. It will be recalled that the repairing of a wall figures there in the story of al-Khidr, and it should above all be recognized that the story of Dhul-Qarnayn concludes with the building of a wall. This Wall of Alexander the Great is, of course, the archetype of a cosmic barrier against dangerous forces to which Hadrian's Wall in some degree corresponds. In another example of the bond between Alexander and al-Khidr, the latter is traditionally understood to guard this wall every night "until the Mahdi appears."[105]

As a planter of trees and a Defender of Nature, "there is a mythic quality of identification

---

104 Cf. *The Red and the White*, page 44.

105 Referenced in *Mysteries of Dune*, page 47; on the Wall of Alexander and other historical examples, see ibid., especially pages 16 and 26-7. In the same work I relate the story of *Twin Peaks* to the Wall of Alexander, and so it is worth noting here that "Glastonbury Grove" in that story is a grove of sycamore trees.

between our King and his land."[106] Specifically, his decades as Prince of Wales and Duke of Cornwall have brought him closer to the Celtic tradition where its traces are strongest in Britain. While rooted in the Christian faith as formulated by the Church of England, King Charles III recommends Islam as the best hope for restoring balance with nature in his realm.[107] It should also not be overlooked that HM The King has presented a specifically Pythagorean perspective in his manifesto *Harmony*, and that the legacy of Pythagoras participates in the Celtic, Christian, and Islamic traditions alike. [108] For that matter, the crowning of the king on what is essentially the cross-quarter day of Spring invites the rapprochement of these three traditions.[109] As we have seen, a true Guardian of the Grail must have knowledge of these three traditions specifically.

No doubt HM The King is a steward of his kingdom, but a steward is properly one who manages that which really belongs to another. The title "Green Man King" testifies that His Majesty Charles Philip Arthur George is under the hidden

---

[106] Aris Roussinos, "The Mythic Power of King Charles III," *UnHerd.com*, 12 September 2022.

[107] See *The Red and the White*, page 55.

[108] On Pythagoreanism and the Celtic tradition, see *Sacred Geography and the Paths of the Sun*, chapter 7. It may be noted that there is a Pythagorean significance to fava beans that were featured in the dish officially chosen for the Coronation celebrations.

[109] Hidrellez, after all, corresponds to Saint George's Day according to Christendom's former calendar; and the sacred geography of Britain testifies that despite modern custom, 1 May is rather too early for the festival of Beltane (see ibid., passim).

authority of al-Khidr, which is hardly more controversial than admitting the living authority of Saint George, patron saint of England and of the Most Noble Order of the Garter. There is, however, a distinction to be made here. Unlike the Christian conception of Saint George, al-Khidr is revered as living unseen on this Earth; and what is more, it is believed that he will remain unseen only "until the Mahdi appears." Time may be symbolized by the face of the Green Man, but it is the expected leader al-Mahdi who is traditionally known as the "Owner" or "Lord of Time (*Sāhib az-Zamān*)." For this reason, the "participation" of al-Khidr in the Coronation proceedings promises more than only a new Carolingian age. The arrival of the Mahdi is, in British terms, the awakening of King Arthur.[110] It is also when the founder of the Qalandars promised to emerge from his mysterious mound once again, for the first time since the era of the Grail legends and Shah Khizr.

If HM King Charles is a steward of al-Khidr, then he too may be associated with the fish, though not necessarily with the Green Man's most distinctive attribute, his immortality. The disclosure of HM The King's cancer diagnosis on 5 February 2024 was obviously new to royal protocol, and while this revelation may serve to help others facing mortality, there is another inevitable significance to

[110] Within the specific setting of the Grail story, Malcolm Godwin relates the Mahdi to the "desired knight" whose arrival brings the healing of the Fisher King (op. cit., page 160.) On al-Mahdi, who is traditionally compared to `Ali and whose function is inseparable from that of Jesus, see *Alchemy in Middle-earth*, *Mysteries of Dune*, and *The Nine Sisters of California*.

this development. The steward king with his affliction recalls the Fisher King of the Grail legend. The specifics of the cancer are a private matter, but in the weeks prior to the announcement of the diagnosis, the public was made aware of King Charles' prostate condition which certainly relates to the region of the Fisher King's wound. The regrettable suffering of His Majesty is simply an indication of the correspondence between himself and the land of Britain; after all, Britain still suffers wrongdoing. Despite the general incomprehension or even resistance to its themes,[111] the Matter of Britain is no longer imaginary. The Arthurian reign of the Green Man King signals that the healing of the land is assured, and what has long been thought to be sleeping is now ready to come to Britain's aid.

---

[111] At Tintagel, a site associated with King Arthur by no less an authority than Geoffrey of Monmouth, the recent installation of a statue named "Gallos" officially downplays this association, offering an alternative image of the past with disdain for the Matter of Britain; nevertheless, the ghostly figure with sword and crown has become popularly known as the "King Arthur Statue."

A contemporary mural in Glastonbury

www.ingramcontent.com/pod-product-compliance
Lightning Source LLC
LaVergne TN
LVHW052355100826
845147LV00013B/845

* 9 7 8 0 9 7 4 1 4 6 8 8 1 *